Celebrating ... of the Oxfam

A review of the history of the annual event that has been raising money for Oxfam since 1967, with anecdotes about some of those who participated, information about **the money raised** and the causes **that were supported**, a look behind the scenes at **the work involved in organising** the walk today, and directions with maps of a dozen of the walks, for walk enthusiasts who might want to retrace past routes.

1983 CAMBRIDGE
OXFAM WALK
Saturday March 5th

For villag
survival
project i
Nepa

For further details cont
Oxfam   your
110 Regent St.   or
Cambridge   represen
Tel: 358758

In aid of  Oxfam

Acknowledgements

We are indebted to the late George Kent, who walked the walks each year and whose essay on the history of the Oxfam Walk forms the basis of the introduction.

This book would not have been possible without the energy and enthusiasm of Carrie Travers, who walked all of the routes featured, wrote the instructions and devised the alternative variations. Please note that the routes described are similar to the original routes but have been adapted to give walks of varying lengths along public rights of way open at the time of going to press.

We are also grateful to the generous co-operation of Chris Elliott of the Cambridge Evening News for allowing access to, and use of, archive material and photographs. We have endeavoured to credit all the photographers whose work we have included and apologise for any mis-attributions or omissions.

Most of all our thanks go to the thousands and thousands of people over the years who have given their time and effort to undertake the walk and raise funds to support such extremely deserving causes.

Celebrating 40 Years of the Oxfam Walk:
compiled and edited by David Cutting with contributions
from George Kent, Carrie Travers and Cecilia Hollick

Published by Cambridge Oxfam Walk Group, © 2007

ISBN: 978 0 9555822 0 2

Design by DCG DESIGN, Cambridge
Maps drawn by David Cutting
Printed by the Burlington Press Limited, Cambridge
Published May 2007
This book is printed on PEFC accredited stock from sustainable and managed forests.

Contents

Photo by Carrie Travers

Discovering Cambridgeshire with the Oxfam walkers

The Oxfam Walk setting off from Cambridge to Bishop's Stortford in 1967

Picture courtesy CEN

The following article was written by the late George Kent, former headmaster of St Bede's School, Cambridge, who participated in the Oxfam Walk each year for 36 years from its inception. This gave him a unique perspective on how the event developed over the years and provides an overview of the walk's history with evocative descriptions of the routes that were used.

In late spring for the past 36 years Oxfam has provided scenic, foot-propelled tours within a radius of 30 miles of Cambridge. Much sponsored money has been raised to help in the Third World countries, but at the same time the walkers have been able to discover, via footpaths and bridleways, a Cambridgeshire far from gaudy supermarkets and the camera-clicking tourists of King's Parade.

"... the first two walkers carrying an Oxfam banner, Paul Wolfe and Colin Burlton, both Cambridge students, crossed the river to lead the way to Trumpington Road and the A11.

Each walker has been sponsored by one or more people who have agreed to pay Oxfam a sum of money for each mile covered. The sums range from three-pence per mile to 12s 6d."

Excerpt from the Cambridge Evening News report, 22/04/67, on the first Oxfam walk from Cambridge to Bishop's Stortford.

1,300 off on the great Oxfam walk

A human snake consisting of more than 1,300 people stretched from Newnham to the Shelford borders of Cambridge today as walkers of all nationalities set out to raise £7,800 for Oxfam Indian aid.

Their destination was Bishops Stortford, 27 miles away, and the organisers were expecting first arrivals at about 3 p.m.

Soon after 8 a.m. the walkers began massing on Lammas Lane, Newnham. By 8.45 a.m. ~und~ had been through ~~~~ desk and ~~~ ready ~~

Cambridge Evening News report of 22/04/67

The first walkers to reach Bedford were a group of four, including last year's first home, the Cambridge milkman, Mr Jack Hobart. The others were the president of Cambridge Union Society, Mr Patrick Tyson-Cain and two undergraduates, Mr Chris Nicholls, of Fitzwilliam College and Mr David Turnbull, of St John's.

The first Oxfam walks in 1967, 1968 and 1969 were one way, long distance routes on dusty and noisy main roads, without much scope or time to observe the countryside hidden behind rows of houses or thundering lorries.

On Saturday, 22 April 1967, 1,300 walkers (headed for half a mile by one of the local Parliamentary candidates who then vanished into a phone box in Trumpington) set off on a 32 mile, A130-A11 marathon to Bishop's Stortford. Sponsored long distance walks were relatively new in these parts and clumps of spectators, some offering free refreshments, were to be found in most villages. Outside the straggling approaches to Bishops Stortford was an enterprising professional photographer who asked for a smile from weary walkers and pushed a card into their hands whereby the historic snapshot could be purchased when recovery was complete. The Hockerill Training College complete with mayoral reception party plus a flotilla of Eastern Counties buses marked the end of the marathon.

The Bishop's Stortford route was used again the following year, and then in 1969 a massive switch to the west took place with a 30 miler of concrete and hurtling traffic to Bedford. It had rained for about a month and the fields around Bedford were in flood with cattle clustered together on the higher bits of ground, presumably getting some solace from watching the misfortunes of the human walkers constantly sprayed by

passing vehicles. Various Cambridgeshire dignitaries walked that year, including a future Chief Education Officer who bore on his mud-spattered back a notice stating he was sponsored by Abbotts Travel.

A thousand walk to Bedford, 1969

Picture courtesy CEN

"One walker, who broke all cash records was a 17-year-old pupil of the Leys School, Geh Yang Tek, whose home is in Singapore. He had sponsorship from friends in this country and relatives at home worth £7 3s 9d for every mile he walked, and raised £215 12s 6d."

Excerpt from a report in the Cambridge Evening News, 10/03/69, on the walk from Cambridge to Bedford.

1969 marked the end of one way, long distance road walks for Oxfam. Although fatalities had been avoided, there must have been many requests for following more scenic bridleways and footpaths nearer to home. A circular route of the countryside would also avoid the cost of transporting the walkers back to Cambridge.

North, south, east and west, the Oxfam routes have led away from the city and into the heart of the Cambridgeshire countryside. From the old Brunswick School at 7:00am and past sleeping riverside houses to Stourbridge common where in earlier centuries Europe's largest fair was held; along a deserted towpath with its shattered elms and opposite the grassy slopes of Fen Ditton; then past a pillbox relic of World War II to Baitsbite Lock where early morning fishermen are setting up for the day. North, and under a misty rumbling motorway to Clayhithe, and over the Cam's

Photo by Carrie Travers

The Cam near Bottisham Lock

The publicity flier for the walk in 1979.

lowest bridge to the east bank footpath which passes the wooden barn where the WRVS in battle array have dispensed spam sandwiches and first aid to the walkers.

An early, two-carriage train shuttles along the western horizon from Ely to Cambridge, and the earth is darker with a rich scent of root crops rising in the dawn. The white paint of Bottisham Lock gleams ahead and marks a choice of Oxfam routes. The North-west circuit lies along the metal strip road past chained Alsatians on guard at a scrap merchant's property to the remoteness of New Farm, Heron Farm, and Joist Fen. The earth is even blacker now, and once or twice a lonely heron is seen in the stillness of the fields near the banked river. The old (120 tons of water a minute) pumping station of Stretham and the village spire lie ahead, and beyond them on a clear day can be seen Ely Cathedral, the queen of the desolate fens, seeming to give purpose and encouragement to all life within her realm.

West, through thick mud paths of Undertaker's Fen and across the old West River; past Australia Farm usually shrouded in mist and drizzle to the solitude of Bedlam Farm with the shelter of Haddenham Ridge to the north. Wind-

Photo by Carrie Travers

Aldreth Causeway

Photo by Mike Crofts

The Chilford Walk

swept walkers toil across the reed bowed and oozing fens unnoticed except by a lonely tractor and the hardy cattle at pasture.

The village of Aldreth is the site of the Norman Belsar's struggles to build a floating bridge to invade the island of Ely and finally defeat Hereward. The village also marks the Oxfam turning point back to the city life of the south via the thickness of Smithey Fen and onto hard concrete and paving at Twentypence Road. Then the long, long walk through the once famous cheese village of Cottenham with its mixture of country cottages, mini super-markets, housing estates, dusty war memorial, and fading Georgian houses – to a final checkpoint in Cambridge.

Some years ago Oxfam routes from Bottisham lock veered NE along the raised coprolite bank beside the Cam with the more pastured and populated areas of the Swaffham and Adventurers' Fen to the right. Isolated farms nestle in clumps of trees with less windswept cattle ambling through the riverside pastures. On the southern horizon stands the windmill of Swaffham and the outskirts of Bottisham where Charles I hid one night over 300 years ago.

Nearing Upware, where seagoing ships once unloaded in sight of Ely Cathedral on the skyline above,

82-year-old Fellow takes 25 miles in his stride

He may be 82 but Dr. Archibald Clark-Kennedy, of Grange Road, Cambridge, proved that he was just as good as the other 778 competitors and one donkey when it came to completing a 25-mile cross country sponsored walk round the city for Oxfam at the weekend.

A Fellow of Corpus Christi College, he estimates that he has raised more than £50 for an activity he has been supporting ever since the annual walk was started.

"I enjoy the exercise and don't have to do any special training," he commented. "It keeps me fit and is something I just do in my stride."

The walk's organisers hope to raise between £5,000 and £6,000 from a turn-out which was about 150 more than last year's figure.

Excerpt from a report in the Cambridge Evening News, 8/03/76.

Picture: Tony Jedrej courtesy Cambridge Evening News

Youngsters from Comberton Village College stepping out in 1990. They chose the middle distance of the three options (10 miles) round the Wandlebury Estate.

the footpath becomes less tangled and many pleasure boats are at mooring. Metal strip roads lead a variety of ways into the ancient kingdom of Reach perched on the distant hillside. A lonely telephone box stands half a mile from habitation and gives pause for thought as to its placing and usage.

The Lode leads through thick peat to the twisting lanes and cottages of the old Hythe of Reach, and thence to the wide village green with two rows of houses in straight lines on either side petering out as the Devil's Dyke suddenly enters the village. Reach Fair on the holiday Monday before Ascension Day once marked the importance of this ancient port with its Royal Charter enabling various modern 'Monarchs' to claim the kingship of the area. 'King Len' who ran the village shop and post office in the 1960s was the last of this blue-blooded line stretching back to King John himself.

South-east now along the Devil's Dyke sometimes 60ft above the ground with clunch-quarried Burwell to the left and the hum of motorway traffic somewhere ahead. It rains usually about now, sharp, stinging rain from the east as if a reminder from those ancient earthwork builders that their Dyke will stand long after the new motorway has crumbled and gone.

A bridge over the A45 and then down along chalky

tracks and paths to the gentler lands of the Wilbrahams and refreshments at the village school with cardboard protecting the polished floors from Oxfam muddy boots. Then into Fulbourn Fen with the Pasque flowers of Fleam Dyke in spring, and over a single line rail crossing manned by a waterproofed undergraduate complete with umbrella, deckchair and study books. He gives an encouraging watery nod in the direction of Cambridge soon reached via Fulbourn village, the Ida Darwin and Cherry Hinton.

Some Oxfam routes to the east have started at St Bede's School and led through to Teversham with its early English church and under the A45/A14 culvert to Honey Hill, Snout Corner, and Horningsea once linked by ferry to Milton. Through Stow cum Quy Fen to that old railway line that passes silently round the back of Anglesey Abbey where Augustinian monks once walked through what are now 100 acres of ornamental gardens. Swaffham Bulbeck marks the turn for home as it did for many tired warehousemen in the 1700s after a long day's work at the busy shipping wharf of Commercial End at the head of Swaffham Bulbeck Lode. Then along chalky farm tracks round Bottisham, and ahead the spires of Cambridge on the horizon.

Oxfam routes leading west from Cambridge usually start at Newnham School or Selwyn Diamond and follow the misty footpath through Grantchester meadows where monks from Ely searched in the ruins of early Cambridge for a stone coffin for St Etheldreda. Wood smoke marks Grantchester's early risers, and a girl on horseback follows the bridleway which leads over the M11 and is silhouetted high above the beginning of the day's motorised rat race.

The western paths and tracks lead round and over, and down and up the rolling arable and wooded land of this part of Cambridgeshire. Past the wood frame and thatched village of Barton, of ancient archery fame, to Comberton where cottage dwellings have now grown to opulence with 2/3 cars in

Umuganda
FOR RWANDA

'rearing weeds from a road - men and women in Rwanda doing their Umuganda   *Photo: Jo Hopkins/Oxfam*

on the OXFAM
CAMBRIDGE WALK
SAT. 12th MAY

The publicity flier for the walk in 1990.

Picture: Roger Adams courtesy Cambridge Evening News

George Kent and Nathan Paulson lead the way in 1995.

"More than 800 dedicated walkers turned out for the 28th annual Oxfam sponsored walk to fund projects to protect people in the Amazon.

Excited Nathan Poulson, five, could not wait to take part in his first Oxfam walk ... Giving him some advice was veteran walker George Kent, 67, who has taken part in every sponsored Oxfam walk since 1967."

Excerpt and picture from the Cambridge Evening News, 15/05/95.

the driveways. The newcomers have yet to bury completely the old village of pigeon houses, Herring Field which once fed the poor in Lent, and the causeway leading to St Mary's church. The pre-Christian village maze lies at peace under the tarmac of the infant school playground.

Farmland tracks lead past the giant radio telescopes of Lords Bridge searching for footsteps on other galaxies, and head towards the winding cottaged villages of the Eversdens. Cattle amble towards a gate hoping that the early morning passer-by has brought an unexpected breakfast to warm their damp and steamy bodies. Steep chalky paths are soon forgiven once the skyline is reached and a land at peace lies all around. One or two tractors are beginning a weekend's overtime, and a field of young spring wheat waves downwards towards Orwell with its vast clunch pit, giving a whitewashed if precipitous approach to the village. The sloping path leads softly through the churchyard and down to the village High Street where once stood a gigantic maypole on the meridian of Greenwich. Then eastwards through

Wilsmere Down Farm with its ever anxious guard dog, and to Barrington of lengthy village green and great smoking chimneys. A rest point in the village school, then across windswept fields, once the forested domain of prehistoric animals to the banks of the Cam with a sign saying 'Don't fall in' at the edge of the river footpath.

Round the village of Haslingfield with two small boys fishing on a bridge, and beneath the site of the ancient pilgrim's shrine on the top of White Hill with its views of Ely to the north and Dunstable to the south. North-east past the riding school, away to Cantelupe Farm with the village of Grantchester reposing amidst trees beyond the now flashing motorway using up enough petrol in a day to pay for much of a Third World project.

The majority of Oxfam walks through the years have explored the west of Cambridgeshire possibly because of the wide choice of footpaths and bridleways enabling a scenic circuit to be devised without the danger of too

Photo by Carrie Travers

Barrington

Hildersham

Photo by Carrie Travers

Rivey Hill

Photo by Mike Crofts

many main roads. One western route lies along the ancient ridgeway from Coton where the church terrace revealed the remains of a prehistoric mammoth woolly rhinoceros. Then to Hardwick where the church was purified in 1643 for three half-pence, and on to Highfields. Paths lead south to Toft, Bourn, Kingston, Wimpole Hall (base of a number of recent Oxfam walks thanks to the National Trust), and the village of New Wimpole created imperiously in the late 1700s when the first Earl of Hardwick, the owner of the Hall, decided that the servants' cottages should not lower the dignity of his residence and had them rebuilt out of eyeshot.

Kings and Queens of England are not neglected on Oxfam Walks: Madingley's redbrick Tudor Hall was where Edward VII 'lodged' when a Cambridge undergraduate; Charles I was interviewed by Cromwell and Fairfax in 1647 at Childerley Hall near Dry Drayton; Longstanton can boast that Elizabeth I 'slept here' which she did in 1564 at the Bishop's Palace – but she did not retire to rest until she had dispatched some student actors into the dark of night for attempting to perform a blasphemous play; a grateful Henry III gave Rampton to Robert de Lisle who built a Fort, Giant's Hill, for protection from the 'the natives'; and Queen Victoria stayed one night at Wimpole Hall, and was not too 'amused' at the lateness of the revels in the hall beneath her bedchamber.

The main Roman routes through Cambridgeshire are found in part on most Oxfam walks: the Icknield Way, Ermine Street, Akeman Street, Watling Street and the Via Devana. The latter Roman trek started one year at the High School for Boys (now Hills Road Sixth Form College) and wormed its way round the back of the then minute New Addenbrooke's Hospital, and via Worts Causeway towards Fulbourn with a right turn at the top of the hill and onto the track which leads past the beech woods of Wandlebury with its ancient triple-ringed earthworks and the grave of the first Arab stallion brought to this country. The Gogs mark the highest point of Cambridgeshire – 220 feet above sea level with the next highest point to the east being the Ural mountains of Russia some miles away.

George Kent and Cecilia Hollick, two people who have made an enormous contribution to the history of the Oxfam Walk. George participated in every walk from its inception to 2003 and supported it in so many ways. Cecilia has been involved with the walk for the past ten years and been the walk co-ordinator since 2002. Her extraordinary industriousness and enthusiasm have been instrumental in the survival of the walk as an annual event.

The Via Devana is a straight path through wooded countryside with ups and downs and many puddles in spring. Horseheath and West Wickham mark the return routes via outlying farm tracks of Balsham and the prickly remnants of Fleam Dyke with the ancient Saxon meeting place of Mutlow Hill to the left.

Since the walk's inception more than 40,000 nameless Oxfam Walkers have found much of Cambridgeshire's peace and beauty. They have raised well over half a million pounds; and all ages, shapes and sizes have shared the joys and travails of a common cause.

George Kent

Courtesy Cambridge Evening News

Forty years of fundraising: work in progress

After decades of sponsored events and high profile fundraising in the full glare of national and international publicity, such methods for raising money and awareness have become commonplace and it is easy to forget that back in 1967 when Oxfam organised a walk from Cambridge to Bishop's Stortford, it was still something of a novelty. The fact that 1,300 people had agreed to walk 27 miles, mostly along a busy main road – described by the Cambridge Evening News at the time as "probably the largest trek in the history of Cambridge" – was a remarkable event not to be underestimated.

This set a trend and established a formula that has stood the test of time and shown the way to many other charities and worthy causes. Organising an event that invited participation and commitment not only engaged a large number of people who were prepared to reward the efforts of the participants but also played a significant role in raising awareness of important issues of poverty and deprivation.

In that first year of the walk over £7,000 was raised. The local Oxfam organiser, Mr Eric Fisher, in a report in the Cambridge Evening News in June 1967, said that "in my wildest dreams I did not think that a figure approaching anywhere near the target of £7,800 would ever be achieved."

In fact, the following year the walk reached its target of £10,000, with the money going towards a soil conservation scheme to help in a cattle-rearing area in Botswana. A similar target was reached the following year, when more than 1,000 people braved the busy road to Bedford to help raise money towards providing three houses in a South American children's village.

After 1969 the walk became less of a route march and more of a countryside ramble, involving more footpaths and less roads, with routes taking walkers back to where they started and offering a choice of distance. In one report, an organiser claimed that "it is very inconvenient to organise a walk which is not on the roads, because you cannot reach the walkers with medical aid or refreshments by car." Clearly organising such an event was a learning process and there wasn't a template readily available; the Oxfam walk was designing the template.

By 1971 there was talk of the walk being cancelled. The walk organiser, Mr Paul Kirkley, said that no one had been found to organise the walk the following year and that it took an awful lot of time to organise. Already the numbers particpating had dropped

below 1,000 and the proceeds from the 1970 walk had dipped to £6,000.

However, it did survive and this section looks at how the aims of the walk evolved and at the causes which have benefited from the funds raised.

In July 1973, the Oxford News reported that despite torrential rain, 1,200 turned up for a 28-mile Oxfam walk in Cambridge. All but 200 finished the course. The organisers hoped to top the previous year's total of £7,500. The money was to go to an orphanage and rehabilitation centre in Vietnam and a school in Ethiopia.

By lunchtime most of the walkers were soaked to the skin by the torrential rain. Scores gave up but others carried on regardless of the soaking – and a liberal covering of mud. Those who gave up were returned by cars and minibuses to the walk centre at Newnham.

For those who fancied an alternative to walking, there was a five-mile punt race from Cambridge to Grantchester. More than a dozen crews, sponsored at about £10 each, took part.

In 1974 the publicity was directed towards raising money for well drilling in Ethiopia. In the previous October Jonathan Dimbleby, in a renowned television broadcast, had brought to the public's attention the plight of the Ethiopians, who had suffered a terrible drought that killed thousands. After the initial aid had been rushed in what was needed was a well-drilling programme to provide water supplies for some of the villages, not to mention medical aid and help for farmers to rebuild their lives.

1978
CAMBRIDGE
OXFAM WALK
SATURDAY 29 APRIL
FOR PROJECTS IN
INDIA

CONTACT
YOUR SCHOOL OR COLLEGE REP:
or
OXFAM
110 regent street
cambridge   tel: 58758

Publicity produced for the years of 1983, 1984 and 1988.

Unfortunately the walk met with misfortune when a young girl of 13, Ruth Carpenter, was hit by a car in Trumpington and was sent to Addenbrookes with a suspected fractured skull. Although the accident did not occur through negligence or lack of organisation, there were calls from the police for an end to all sponsored walks because "of the risks involved". There was a spate of letters in the pages of the Cambridge Evening News on the issue but the event survived the trauma and the 1974 walk raised £8,430 for Oxfam GB.

The walkers in March 1986 who braved the elements raised over £24,000 – a record at that time.

Picture courtesy CEN

In the following years Ethiopia was still a cause supported by the walk, joined by food crises around the world in India and Bangladesh, and projects as far afield as Guatemala, Tanzania, Brazil, Vietnam and Nepal.

The numbers of walkers and the sums raised took a dip in the late seventies, with walkers numbering around 600 – 700 and funds raised reportedly around £5- 6,000. However, by the early eighties the organisers were becoming more ambitious, with aims of raising over £10,000 each year.

The publicity for the Walk in 1983, told the prospective walkers, "in the Shivapuri area of Nepal the soil is almost infertile, the water supplies are poor and widespread erosion is adversely affecting the climate. Recently there has been a severe drought and an acute foodgrain shortage. The shrinking of forests has removed the villagers' final source of income and they are faced with dreadful misery. To help alleviate the desperate situation, the Village Redevelopment Project has been set up to show the villagers how

LOOKING TO A GREENER FUTURE?

Help us to help them and their families fight off famine for ever: RE-GREEN ETHIOPIA!

on the OXFAM CAMBRIDGE WALK
Saturday 11 May 1991

With **20, 10** and 4 mile routes to choose from, **the Walk caters for all:** the athletic, the less energetic, the young and the not-so. Walk by yourself, or - still better - with friends and families. However you do it, remember it's for sponsorship, so get plenty of pledges before the day and collect the money quickly afterwards. If you can't walk, why not offer to be a steward or marshal on the day? (You could even get sponsored for that!)

Walk for a Fairer World

Saturday 9th May 1992

Sponsored Anniversary Walk

on the 25th Oxfam Cambridge Walk

OXFAM — Working for a Fairer World

In the 1990s, publicity material adopted the trend towards increased use of colour, but some things didn't seem to change – Ethiopia was back on the agenda. In 1992, fundraisers received a certificate congratulating them on their efforts in raising funds for the Oxfam Wollayta Village Project in Ethiopia. Design of publicity was becoming more sophisticated, marketing more professional and corporate sponsorship was introduced.

Oxfam Walk for Fair Trade

Sunday 9th May 1993
The Oxfam Cambridge Sponsored Walk for Fair Trade

OXFAM — Working for a Fairer World

Walk for India

David Cutting Graphics

THE BURLINGTON PRESS

Saturday 21 May 1994
★ Join the 27th OXFAM
Cambridge Sponsored Walk

Chance to win a Walking Holiday!

Setting off in 1990.

Publicising the 1997 walk.

Picture courtesy CEN

to improve crop production and livestock, set up other methods of generating income, improve health and nutrition and to provide a school."

In 1986 the walk achieved record funds of £24,000 and by 1988, the 21st anniversary of the Oxfam Walk, organisers were claiming that £350,000 had been raised by the event since 1967. That year the sponsorship money went to three aid schemes in Brazil: a social organisation which encouraged co-operative groups and helped them to defend their rights; helping fishermen near San Luis to defend their interests; and a market gardening scheme encouraging vegetable production for family use.

The following year the focus had switched across the world to Bangladesh, with money going to help train and organise landless families to claim their rights to

'Khas Land' which they could use to farm and harvest their own food.

In the 1990s the fundraising stepped up a gear. Design of publicity became more sophisticated, marketing was more professional and corporate sponsorship was introduced. The 1998 event, with its starting point at Wimpole Hall, was now offering a range of attractions to tempt the public into participating, such as a helicopter from Burman Aviation, a face painter and foot massagers. Prizes were on offer for those raising the most sponsorship, including a walking holiday and a free helicopter flying lesson. The walk set a new record with 1,435

Joan Lintott, second from left, who had taken part in the Oxfam Walks for 20 years, with organisers Lucy Palourti, Serina Rolph and Lucy Moses in 1998.

walkers taking part and there were ambitions to beat the £35,000 which had been raised in 1997.

The total funds raised since the walk's inception was, according to a press release issued prior to the 1999 walk, over half a million pounds. Whether or not this could be verified, and just who was counting, is not clear, but there was no getting away from the fact that the Oxfam Walk had raised a tremendous amount of money for good causes and was now an established institution, an integral part of the Cambridge calendar. Lucy Palourti, Oxfam Campaigns executive officer, was quoted in a report in the Cambridge Town Crier saying that in 1999 1,971 walkers had raised more than £45,000, which beat all previous records. The venue was Chilford Hall and the attractions on offer outdid previous years and included fairground rides, face painters, a jive band, the Ian Vickery tribute Band and a giant game of snakes and ladders, supported by Cambridge MP Anne Campbell, who played with children from Neale-Wade Community College.

In a competition run by Oxfam to devise a board game that could be used in schools to educate children on the plight of the Third World, six students from the Neale-Wade Community College in March won first prize – a residential activity holiday at Finborough Hall in Suffolk.

A particularly interesting feature of the 1999 walk was the support for Oxfam's campaign 'Education Now'. A mock classroom, with desks, chairs and a blackboard (remember them?) was set up at Chilford Hall and walkers were encouraged to draw and sign their own footprints as part of a petition to be presented to Gordon Brown to demand primary education for all through increased debt relief to poor countries.

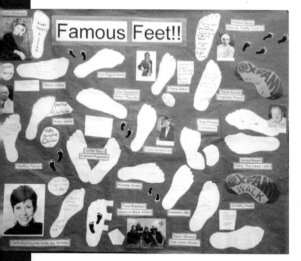

Cambridge United players gave their support – and their footprints – to the 1999 Education Now campaign. The team signed a petition and the giant yellow boot was presented to Chancellor Gordon Brown. The Oxfam team featured here are, from front to back, Kate Bingley, Lucy Moses and Jessie Monk.

Competitions for the most money raised (with prizes as incentives) had by now become a common feature of the walks. In 2000, a thirteen-year-old, Leo Kitchen, won the prize of a classic walking holiday for his efforts in raising £793 and the corporate team challenge was won that year by employees of PriceWaterhouseCoopers who had raised a record-breaking £1,419. The theme of that year was support for the campaign to drop Third World debt and the 'On the Line' project, which aimed to link people living in the eight countries along the Greenwich Meridian Line. One of the poorest of those countries, Burkino Faso in West Africa, was heavily indebted to multilateral institutions and was spending more money on debt repayment than on healthcare and education. With only one in five adults able to read, the cycle of poverty would continue unless it could be broken by the cancellation of the debts. The walk was

reported to have raised a staggering £46,000 in total.

The following year, 2001, the entire future of the Oxfam Walk was put in potential jeopardy when Oxfam announced plans to close its Cambridge Office. The regional campaigns manager, Julian Jacobs, was reported as saying, "we were concerned that the walk may not survive this change. It has become an extremely complex event, absorbing a huge amount of staff and volunteer time." The walk was by now Oxfam's largest local sponsored fundraising event in the UK, regularly attracting 1,500 participants and raising tens of thousands of pounds.

To the great credit of the people of Cambridge and, in particular, Cecilia Hollick, who took on the role of team co-ordinator, a team of determined volunteers rallied round. Despite this, the walk suffered an even greater setback with the outbreak of foot and mouth disease which swept the country and the walk was abandoned for the first time in its 34-year history.

However, in 2002 it was back on the agenda, now run by volunteers with support from Oxfam Head Office, and reportedly raised £37,000. Corporate sponsors like the Co-operative Group and Stagecoach were ready to give their support as were celebrities who helped publicise the launch.

The walk in 2004 started at Chilford Hall and Bruce Kent, honorary vice-president of the Campaign for Nuclear Disarmament, together with his brother George and Cecilia Hollick, stalwarts of the event, helped launch the appeal at Lammas Land, Cambridge, the site of the start of the first walk in 1967. This year saw the introduction of an explicit target – £50 – for each participant to aim to raise. The organisers were hoping to collect £50,000 for Oxfam's Emergencies Fund. The following year individuals were again asked to aim to raise at least £50 each, again for the Emergencies Fund.

Oxfam responds to over 40 emergencies worldwide every year. The winter of 2003 had seen thousands of families left homeless by the earthquake in Iran and in 2004 people had seen vast areas of south-east Asia devasted by the tsunami. There was a pressing need to establish clean water supplies and packs of oral re-hydration salts to save the lives of hundreds of children suffering from diarrhoea.

The next year saw the horrific earthquake in Kashmir and more terrible famines in Africa. In addition to the immediate response needed for such crises there is a great deal of long-term rebuilding and restoration of infrastructure required. The events come and go in our news bulletins but the suffering does not end when they are no longer the focus of our attention. Oxfam is there for the long haul, doing vital work, saving lives and communities. The £50,000 which the Oxfam Walk aims to raise each year for Oxfam GB makes a huge contribution to this humanitarian endeavour.

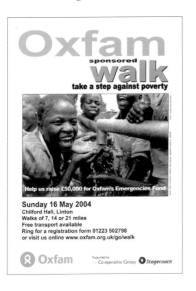

Oxfam sponsored walk
take a step against poverty

Help us raise £50,000 for Oxfam's Emergencies Fund

Sunday 16 May 2004
Chilford Hall, Linton
Walks of 7, 14 or 21 miles
Free transport available
Ring for a registration form 01223 502798
or visit us online www.oxfam.org.uk/go/walk

Oxfam   Supported by Co-operative Group Stagecoach

Routes and Maps of 12 walks

In this section we take a closer look at 12 of the routes that Oxfam has devised in the past 40 years. Our selection represents the complete range of areas of Cambridgeshire where walks have been organised and illustrate the great variety of possibilities available to those keen on walking.

In some years Oxfam was given special permission, for the event only, to use paths on private land. Other permissive paths have since been closed. Over the years roads have become much busier and the early walks were longer than the weekend rambler might want to do. For these reasons, for some of the years, variations to the original routes have been proposed and these changes are identified with brown text.

The maps in the book show you each route at a glance. Below is a key for the conventions used in these maps. All the routes have been revisited prior to publication so the detailed instructions are as up-to-date as we could manage. Nevertheless, we advise walkers to take an OS Explorer map with them and the appropriate map is identified in the headings at the top of each route.

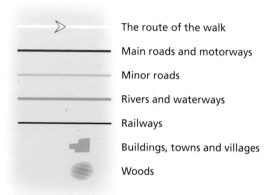

The route of the walk

Main roads and motorways

Minor roads

Rivers and waterways

Railways

Buildings, towns and villages

Woods

1974

NEWNHAM – GRANTCHESTER – WANDLEBURY – FULBOURN – FLEAM DYKE – BALSHAM – LINTON

Distance   26 miles (or 16 miles or 12 miles)
Map   OS Explorer 209

The 1974 walk, held on 9 March, began and ended at Newnham Croft School. The walk was organised for a 7.00am start and walkers were asked to leave no later than 10.00am so that they would be back before dusk. Here we also offer two shorter alternatives – starting at Wandlebury and either returning to Wandlebury (16 miles) or finishing at Linton and catching a bus (12 miles).

The Roman Road

The first 5 miles

To repeat the original walk, begin at Newnham, go through Grantchester Meadows to Grantchester then to Trumpington. From Anstey Way take the path across the fields to Red Cross Lane. Cross over the A1307 and turn into Worts Causeway. At the end take the road to **Fulbourn**. At the top of the hill turn right onto the Roman Road and walk along the Roman Road for about a mile to join the 16-mile loop which begins at Wandlebury. (If you've walked this stage, now skip to ☛ in the following text.)

16-mile loop from Wandlebury or 12 miles Wandlebury to Linton, returning by bus

Car parking at Wandlebury, 'pay and display'. Note the time the gate closes.

Bus No 13, Cambridge – Haverhill, via Linton, stops at Wandlebury.

From **Wandlebury** car park go up the hill to the pond. With woods on your left go down to the way-marked track bearing left between fields. By the house in the woods turn left to the Roman Road bridle path and turn right after the kissing-gate ☛.

After about ½ mile turn left between black and white posts. The track leads to a very, quiet, straight tarmac road to **Fulbourn**, with a windmill to your left. Cross the road at the end into School

Lane. At the thatched cottage bear right along Ludlow Lane. At the War Memorial turn right and then left into Stonebridge Lane which continues as a bridleway. Turn left at a 6-barred green metal gate, along a sign-posted public footpath. Where the tracks cross, turn right, along a narrower path towards the **Fleam Dyke**. Climb the steps and enjoy Fleam Dyke for the next 3 miles, crossing the A11 by footbridge. Near the Olde Farmhouse follow the way marks carefully.

Wandlebury

Near the 'Ambush' take the way-marked route to the right. Go up the wooden steps and bear left diagonally towards a group of young trees, over a wooden stile, through the trees and across a large field. You can see the Linton water-tower to the right. Go through a gap in the hedge, cross a field towards a concrete water tower on the horizon. At a wide track go through a way-marked gap in the hedge towards houses just visible through trees. Go across the field, a wooden bridge and two more fields. At the overhead cables turn left to join the Icknield Way. Almost immediately turn right past a block of four garages on your left, taking the path on the right-hand side of the field. Go through a metal kissing gate and turn right through a gate after a water trough. Follow Nine Chimneys Lane until you reach **Balsham** High Street.

Turn left up the High Street and at the thatched butcher's shop turn right into Woodhall Lane.

(If you have a largish dog with you or to avoid awkward stiles follow this track for just over a mile until you reach the Harcamlow Way (Roman Road) Turn right and rejoin the other routes at ☞ below.)

Otherwise, after ½ mile, continue between two hedges. After a few hundred yards turn right over a wooden bridge and then immediately left. Go over three stiles, along a short path between trees and turn left across the field aiming for Linton water tower. At a wide gap in the hedge you meet the Harcamlow Way (Roman Road).

☞ **For the 16-mile route** turn right and follow the Roman Road for about 6 miles back to Wandlebury.

For the 26-mile route return to Wandlebury along Roman Road and then to Newnham.

For the 12-mile route cross the Roman Road and continue across two fields, turning left at the B1052. Walk first along the road and then up the track to the Linton water tower. Turn right after the water tower and follow the track along and down into **Linton**. Turn right at the first road and then left into Crabtree Croft. After the path goes between two fences you come to Symonds Lane. Turn left, past Hill Way. When Symonds Lane meets the High Street cross to the bus stop opposite.

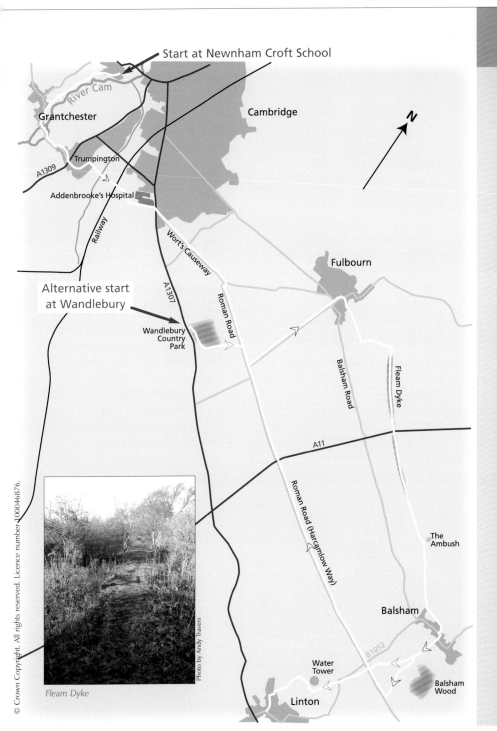

Start at Newnham Croft School

River Cam

Grantchester

Cambridge

N

A1309

Trumpington

Addenbrooke's Hospital

Railway

Wort's Causeway

Fulbourn

Alternative start at Wandlebury

A1307

Roman Road

Wandlebury Country Park

Balsham Road

Fleam Dyke

A11

Roman Road (Harcamlow Way)

The Ambush

Balsham

B1052

Water Tower

Balsham Wood

Fleam Dyke

Photo by Andy Travers

Linton

1975

JESUS GREEN – HORNINGSEA – CLAYHITHE – UPWARE – STRETHAM – HADDENHAM – RAMPTON – HISTON

Distance 27½ miles
Maps OS Explorer 209, 225, 226

In order to minimise road walking and to avoid inaccessible parts, variations to the route of 1975 have been made and are shown in brown type.

Jesus Green, Cambridge to Bottisham Lock (6 miles)

From Jesus Green, walk beside the river on Midsummer Common, along Riverside to the foot-bridge on Stourbridge Common. Cross and turn right, following the Fen Rivers Way path, to rejoin the riverbank at the Penny Ferry, **Chesterton**. Continue on the Fen Rivers Way to Bottisham Lock, crossing the road-bridge at **Clayhithe**.

Bottisham Lock to Haddenham (12 miles)

At Bottisham Lock cross to the left bank of the river and follow the Fen Rivers Way way-marks for approximately 6 miles. From **Upware** you can catch glimpses of Ely Cathedral ahead. The path crosses the A1123 and after about a mile reaches the Fish and Duck Marina. Go over the green footbridge, the West River Bridge. Turn left and go

Baites Bite Lock

Photos by Carrie Travers

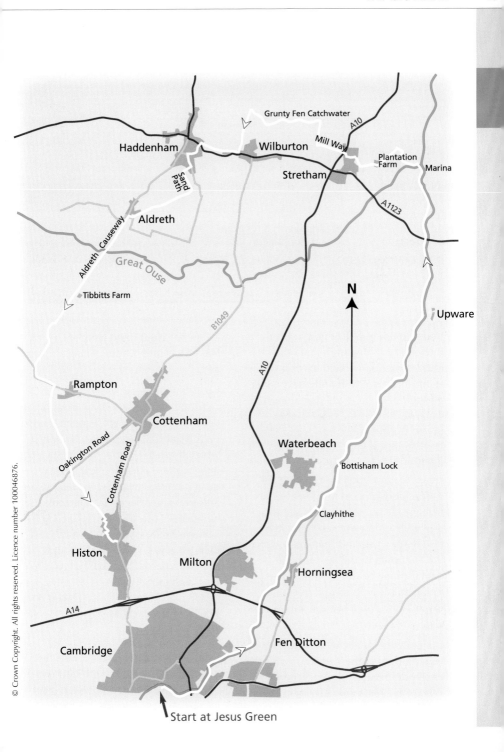

Grunty Fen Catchwater

A10

Haddenham

Mill Way

Wilburton

Stretham

Plantation Farm

Marina

Sand Path

A1123

Aldreth

Aldreth Causeway

Great Ouse

N

Tibbitts Farm

B1049

Upware

Rampton

Oakington Road

A10

Cottenham

Waterbeach

Bottisham Lock

Cottenham Road

Clayhithe

Histon

Milton

Horningsea

A14

Cambridge

Fen Ditton

Start at Jesus Green

The Cam near Bottisham Lock

under the railway bridge, Holt Fen Bridge. Duck! Bear right after the bridge and follow the track as it bends right. Turn sharp left at the way-mark post and left again when you reach the concrete track, which you should follow through the farmyard of Plantation Farm. Turn left, as way-marked, towards **Stretham**. When the concrete track ends turn right at the public footpath sign to go up and through the cemetery. Bear left and downhill at Berry Green. Turn right into Berry Close and then left towards the windmill. In the far left-hand corner of the cul-de-sac follow the footpath to Ely Road and turn right towards the A10 *which you need to cross with extreme care.*

Go along the public byway, Mill Way, turning right at the T-junction of tracks, onto the Black Fen Waterway Track, Parsons Drove. After you cross a deep ditch, turn immediately left to follow the right-hand bank of Grunty Fen Catchwater (drain), along a rough path.

Cross Station Road, Wilburton and continue on the right-hand bank of the drain. When you reach a cream house on the right, turn left onto a byway which leads to Hinton Way. Turn right into Clarkes Lane and right again at the main road towards Haddenham. A little way after the church and some bungalows, turn right immediately before a house called The Haven and then left along a way-marked track beside orchards. This will take you to **Haddenham**.

Haddenham to Histon (9¹⁄₂ miles)

Cross the main road to The Rampart, with the recreation ground on your right. At the end cross and turn right into Duck Lane, turning left into

Photos by Carrie Travers

Aldreth Causeway

first bungalow on the right, cross and turn onto the Public Byway, going straight on along Cuckoo Lane which leads onto another Byway. Continue in this direction for almost 2 miles along Rampton Drift, crossing the Cottenham – Oakington Road at Lambs Cross Farm and going straight on along Gun's Lane. When you reach **Histon** turn right and follow the pavement round, past the church, to the centre of the village.

Bus: Stagecoach, Citi-7 service goes to Cambridge centre and railway station Mon-Sat.

(*The original route followed roads from Histon back to Kings Hedges School.*)

Cherry Orchard. Turn by No 57. Cross into Nelsons Lane, by No 14. At T-junction go right onto footpath which leads to a concrete track. Turn left after a derelict cottage onto Sand Path. As the field boundary bends to the right, go left over the wooden bridge and turn right onto the byway. Continue, with the ditch on your right, towards **Aldreth**.

OS Explorer 225. At the concrete bridge and 30 mph sign to the right, turn left onto a Public Byway following Aldreth Causeway for about ⅔ mile. Cross High Bridge over the Great Ouse River and continue on the Causeway (Track), with trees on your right. After almost a mile, go straight on along the road for 50 yards and then straight on along the Byway. At the next road go right then left onto the Byway, Haven Drove. At the next road turn left towards **Rampton** and walk on the wide grass verge. After the

---

This is an excerpt from the notes given to the walkers in 1975:

Remember the idea of the Walk is to raise money for Oxfam's feeding schemes in the countries worst hit by the current world food crisis, mainly India, Bangladesh and Ethiopia. Please continue trying to get as many sponsors as possible – as well as friends, relatives and neighbours, local firms may be willing to sponsor you. Every little counts! Twenty sponsors at only 2p a mile will raise over £10 if you finish the course!

...Transport will be available back to Cambridge approximately every four miles. Only accept lifts from official Oxfam marshals. Do not go on past a marshal point if you cannot make it to the next one. In case of doubt, you must obey a marshal's decision.

1977

NEWNHAM CAR PARK – GRANTCHESTER – HASLINGFIELD – BARRINGTON – LITTLE EVERSDEN – CALDECOTE – COTON

Distance   25 miles
Map   OS Explorer 209

In order to avoid some road walking, a variation to the route of 1977 has been made and is shown in brown type.

From the car park at Newnham , follow the foot-path signs to **Grantchester** ($1\frac{1}{2}$ miles).

Grantchester to Little Eversden (nearly 9 miles)

Follow the road through Grantchester, with the Orchard Tea-rooms on your left. As the road bends left, turn right at No 48. Take the public footpath, 'Barton 2'. Turn left off the concrete track towards **Haslingfield** and eventually cross the bridge over the M11. Turn right and then left, at a black and white post, away from the motorway. Go through a little wood, over a bridge and continue straight on a long track, Cantelupe Road, for nearly 2 miles to **Haslingfield**. At River Lane, go left towards **Hauxton**. Cross a bridge after about 50 yards and bear right at a fork towards a red-brick bungalow. Continue along the road at Button End. At the junction with Haslingfield Road turn right and just after the bridge turn left at the X-gate, Barrington ($1\frac{1}{4}$ miles). After the fourth

Barrington

Photo by Andy Travers

kissing gate and the bridge, turn left to follow the river round. At the ditch and illegible sign, turn right, keeping to the right-hand bank of the ditch, at the end of which turn left towards the houses of Barrington. Walk over the small level crossing and turn right into Challis Green. At Haslingfield Road cross over to continue on the public bridle-way, Back Lane. Go right through an X-gate, Harlton $1\frac{1}{2}$,

Start at Newnham car park

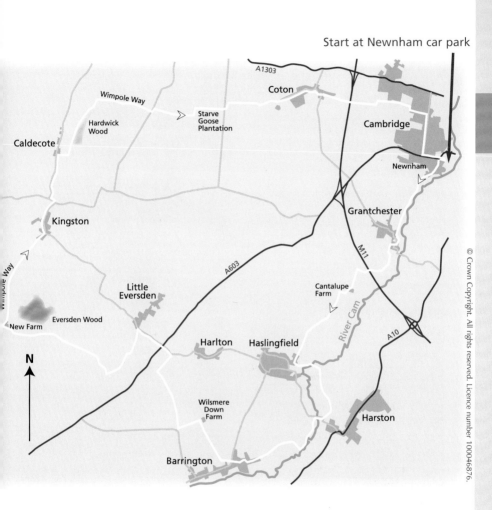

Haslingfield $2^1/_4$. At Wilsmere Down Farm turn left onto a wide track. When you meet the road turn immediately right, taking the track as it goes uphill beside the trees. Follow this track, Whole Way, as it goes downhill and bears right to the road. At the road turn left, cross the staggered junction at the A603 and walk to **Little Eversden**.

Little Eversden to Caldecote (5$^1/_2$ miles)

Take the bridle-way on the left, Mare Way 1, opposite the end of the High Street, Lt. Eversden. Follow the wide track up the hill. At the top turn right onto a wide bridle-path and continue towards the west, passing the Cambridge Water Co. concrete towers to your right. After about another $^1/_2$

Photos by Carrie Travers

Between Haslingfield and Harston

mile there is a wood on your left which the track goes into about 150yds before the road. Turn right at the road and continue to New Farm. Turn right after the second house. About ½ mile along this track, go through a wide gap in the hedge with a bridge behind you and continue in the same direction as before. The hedge is on your left. When you reach the main road through **Kingston,** turn left. The next mile is on roads with no pavement, through the village, across the B1046, left, then right, along Main Street to Carrara Farm, **Caldecote.**

Caldecote to Newnham, Cambridge (8½ miles)

Take the footpath just before Carrara Farm, signed Wimpole Way. Continue along the right-hand edge of the field, turning left at the end of the field. Continue with Hardwick Wood on your right. Cross a wooden bridge and go straight on past railed paddocks on your left. At the end of the paddocks turn right across the fields. You will now be walking east all the way to Cambridge. Carry on until you reach the road into Hardwick. Turn left, cross the road and turn almost immediately right along Port Way. After ⅔ mile, turn left, at a ditch, into Starve Goose Plantation. After a little way turn right to go east, along the right hand edge of the field. Soon you will see Cambridge straight ahead. At the road, cross and turn left. Go down then up and turn right along a signed footpath into woodland. Continue along

Harston

Whitewell Way, with the Firing Range to your right, until you reach **Coton.** The path emerges into a road. Continue along the road. Turn right at the T- junction, into the High Street. At the Plough go down The Footpath, with the recreation ground to the right. There is a footbridge over the M11. The path eventually emerges into Wilberforce Road. Turn right and then left into Adams Road. Walk down to, and turn right along, Grange Road. At the end turn left along the Barton Road and walk back to the car park at Newnham.

1979

HORNINGSEA – LODE – BOTTISHAM FEN – CLAYHITHE

Distance 9½ miles
Map OS Explorer 226

The original walk in 1979 set-off from the then Brunswick School (now Cambridge Regional College), along the river to Fen Ditton and up to Bates Bite Lock. From there it headed east to Stow cum Quy, Little Wilbraham, Great Wilbraham, then looping round to Bottisham, through Bottisham Fen and then joining the River Cam, following the east bank to Clayhithe, then crossing over and continuing along the west bank down past Waterbeach, Horningsea, Chesterton and back to the Brunswick School. (See the route as a white dashed line on the map here.) This route involved a lot of road walking and some sections which were not along public rights of way.

For today's ramblers we propose a 9½-mile walk in a loop starting and finishing at Horningsea, shown in white on the map here. This includes part of the original 1979 route.

If coming by car to **Horningsea**, park just before the verge barriers at the north end of the village.

Walk out of **Horningsea** on the right-hand verge towards Clayhithe and take the footpath to **Lode** 2½ miles. Turn left at the T-junction, by an ash tree. Don't cross the bridge to your left but follow the track bending right until

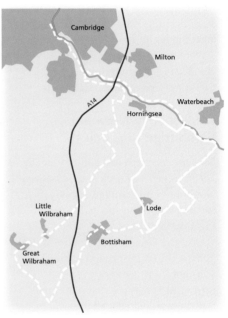

The original 1979 route is shown by a white dashed line and the route featured here is the solid white line.

you reach the pylons. At the tall wooden three-way sign take the direction Lode 1¾ miles with the ditch on your right. After 100 yards, cross a wooden bridge on your right to go through a little woodland (the entrance to Stow cum Quy Fen). Go over a stile and into a field with fine oak trees, keeping near to the right-hand boundary, past two way-mark posts. Enter woodland on the left and

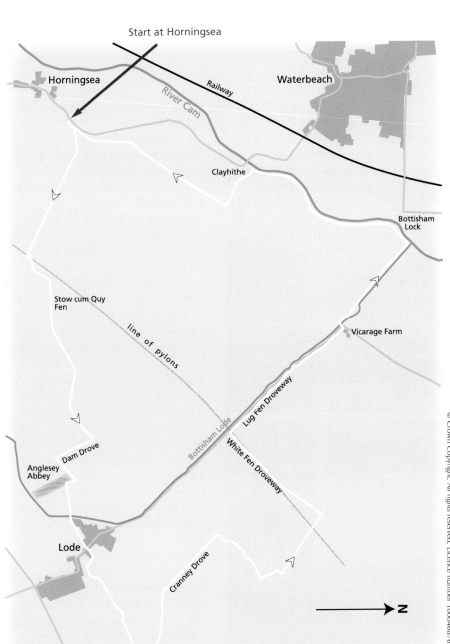

Start at Horningsea

Horningsea

Waterbeach

Railway

River Cam

Clayhithe

Bottisham Lock

Stow cum Quy Fen

line of pylons

Vicarage Farm

Lug Fen Droveway

Bottisham Lode

White Fen Droveway

Dam Drove

Anglesey Abbey

Lode

Cranney Drove

N

go past a long pond, no swimming, on your left. Go over the stile ahead and bear right across to the far side of the field. Go through a metal X-gate and cross a bridge, Lode 1. Walk along the right-hand edge of the field and then along a green lane, between hedges. Half way along turn sharp right. At the end of Dam Drove turn left. Turn right into a belt of trees and after 20 - 30 yards turn left. At the white mill (of **Anglesey Abbey**) go over the bridge and straight ahead along a narrow footpath past allotments. Cross to the road between **Lode** post-office and the church which leads to the recreation ground. Leave by the gap in the opposite hedge. Join a tarmac path between fields and walk towards the houses. At the road turn left and at the bend go straight on past Saxon Farm. Bear left onto the track to Cranney Drove. Bear right at the fork towards pylons on the horizon. At the end of the straight section turn sharp right with the hedge on your right. Do not go through the fence at the end but turn left and continue round the field with the hedge on your right. Do not leave the field until you are facing the pylons. Go straight over a plank bridge and continue on a concrete track under overhead cables. Turn left at the second row of pylons into Sandy Road leading to White Fen Drove. Turn right at the road. Walk along Lug Fen Droveway for over a mile. At Vicarage Farm turn left over the bridge and then right, following the bank of the lode until you reach the River Cam. Go through a X-gate and turn left. Walk past Bottisham Lock and follow the river bank for nearly a mile, along the Fen Rivers Way to **Clayhithe**. Turn left after the information board, before the Conservancy house. Go straight on between the barns. At the Fen Rivers Way sign turn right on the cross-field path, heading towards **Horningsea** on the horizon. Aim for the tree on the opposite side of the field. Carry straight on, going over two stiles, still following the Fen Rivers Way signs through paddocks, through a X-gate and across the next two fields. You will emerge at a big lay-by. Walk along the verge beside the road back to **Horningsea**.

Photos by Andy Travers

Top: Stow cum Quy fen; Below: The Mill at Anglesea Abbey

1989

GREAT SHELFORD – STAPLEFORD – SAWSTON – WHITTLESFORD – GREAT SHELFORD

Distance   12 miles
Map   OS Explorer 209

The 1989 Walk was a round trip of 20 miles starting and finishing at the Sports Pavilion of the Cambridge University Press building off Brooklands Avenue, Cambridge. The route went through parts of Trumpington, Great Shelford and Stapleford, then looped around to Sawston where there was the first refreshment point at about 8 miles. It then passed through Whittlesford to Newton, where there was the second refreshment point at about 13 ½ miles. The last stretch was back through the Shelfords and Trumpington to CUP. The route used a mix of public and private paths, some of which are no longer accessible.

Whittlesford

The route presented here hopefully captures the essence of the original, but starts beyond the city boundaries and is accessible today. The part which is different from the original is in brown text.

Starting at Shelford Station

From Shelford station, Hinton Way, walk up Mingle Lane and along past the church. Almost opposite the road junction, at the end, take a footpath between houses, Vicarage Lane. Turn right along Bar Lane and then left towards Bury Farm on the opposite side of the road. Turn right along the footpath signposted Sawston 2½. Continue on the footpath and after a little over a mile cross the River Granta. Just after a metal X-gate leave the wide track and turn right onto the footpath signed Sawston 1½. When you reach the road, cross and go down Lynton Way, **Sawston**. Turn right at the end before the school and left at the end of the path. Continue along the path at Plantation Road. Turn right and then

Photo by Carrie Travers

left when you reach Green Road. Go right aong the footpath, then left and right into Church Lane. When you reach the end turn left. After 118 Groveland, turn right onto a footpath, between walls. Continue to the bypass. Cross and go over a level-crossing and a white bridge. Go over another bridge and bear left to continue along the road to **Whittlesford** school. From **Whittlesford** school go across the recreation ground to the opposite corner. Cross and turn left into the High Street, walking past the post office. Continue along West End to **Hill Farm Road**. At the junction turn left and after the last house on the left, before the brow of the hill, turn right towards Thriplow 1½. Cross the M11 bridge and continue along the track. About ½ mile from the motorway turn right along a permissive path, just before a ditch. Go through a gap in the hedge and turn right, with the hedge on your right. Near the motorway go left through young trees and follow the path for another ½ mile, going up steps to **Newton Road**. Turn left away from the motorway and follow the road which has grassy verges for nearly a mile until you meet a sharp right turn onto a public bridleway. Follow this track which crosses the motorway about halfway along. At the next road turn left then right onto a public footpath **Sawston** 1½. Leave the field at a way-marked wooden bridge and continue on a narrow path. Go over another wooden bridge and pass a white house immediately to your left. Continue over the river and a level-crossing until a wide track bears

Fern Wood

All Saints Church, Church Street, Little Shelford

left. Turn left at the A1301 past Bridge End Cottage. The pavement bears down to the left as a pedestrian and cycle track. Continue along this to join the road again opposite The Rose pub. Cross the road at the pelican crossing and continue along Church Street to rejoin Mingle Lane, leading back to **Shelford** station.

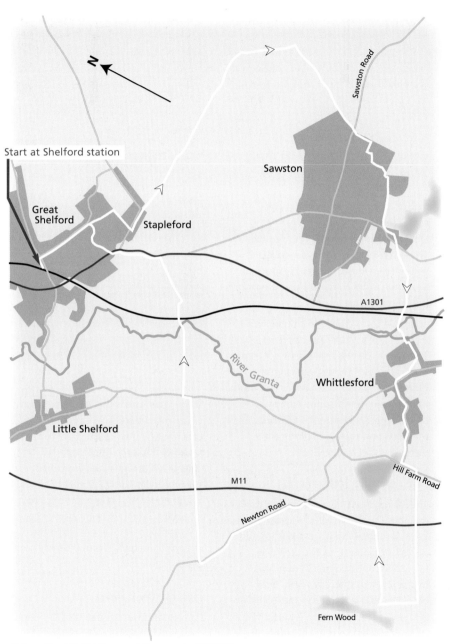

Start at Shelford station

Great Shelford

Stapleford

Sawston

Sawston Road

A1301

River Granta

Whittlesford

Little Shelford

M11

Newton Road

Hill Farm Road

Fern Wood

1991

CAMBRIDGE – COTON – COMBERTON – TOFT – KINGSTON – LITTLE EVERSDEN – HARLTON – HASLINGFIELD – BARTON – GRANTCHESTER – CAMBRIDGE

Distance   4, 10 and 20 miles + a new $8\frac{1}{2}$-mile circular walk from Toft
Map   OS Explorer 209

In 1991 the original routes were 4, 10 and 20 miles from the Selwyn Diamond on Grange Road, Cambridge. These routes are briefly described below followed by a circular route of about $8\frac{1}{2}$ miles from Toft using part of the 20-mile route.

The 4-mile loop

This starts at Selwyn Diamond, Grange Road and goes west to Coton, past The Plough to the Church, where the route follows a footpath south-east approximately beside the Bin Brook to the A603 and then east along the pavement to Grange Road.

The 10-mile loop

The 10-mile loop separates from the 4 mile loop in Coton going out along the Whitewell Way track, to Long Road, north of Comberton. Turn left out of the wood at the road. Go over the bridge and up the rise a little way before turning right onto the track to Starve Goose Plantation where the route turns left towards Comberton. After about $\frac{1}{2}$ mile turn right onto a minor road. There is no pavement for about $\frac{1}{2}$ mile but there is a wide verge.

The Selwyn Diamond, Grange Road, Cambridge

Photo by Andy Travers

At the cross-roads in Comberton turn left towards Barton where you should bear left towards the A603. Cross carefully and take the footpath signposted at the left of a redbrick house. Follow the track east to Grantchester and take the footpath through Grantchester meadows back to Newnham and then back to the Selwyn Diamond, Grange Road, Cambridge.

The 20-mile loop

This separates from the 10-mile loop in Comberton and turns right to Toft, not left to Barton. The route goes to Kingston, along Cranes Lane and the Mare Way to the Eversdens. (This is

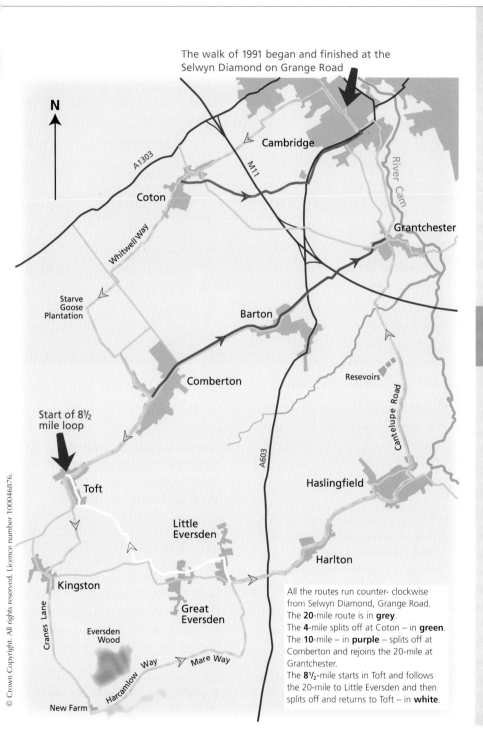

The walk of 1991 began and finished at the Selwyn Diamond on Grange Road

N

Cambridge

A1303

M11

River Cam

Coton

Grantchester

Whitwell Way

Starve
Goose
Plantation

Barton

Comberton

Resevoirs

Cantelupe Road

Start of 8½
mile loop

A603

Haslingfield

Toft

Little
Eversden

Kingston

Harlton

Cranes Lane

Great
Eversden

Eversden
Wood

Harcamlow Way

Mare Way

New Farm

All the routes run counter- clockwise from Selwyn Diamond, Grange Road. The **20**-mile route is in **grey**. The **4**-mile splits off at Coton – in **green**. The **10**-mile – in **purple** – splits off at Comberton and rejoins the 20-mile at Grantchester. The **8½**-mile starts in Toft and follows the 20-mile to Little Eversden and then splits off and returns to Toft – in **white**.

Photo by Andy Travers

Footpath at Little Eversden

described in more detail below) The route then goes east along the road to Haslingfield via Harlton. There is no pavement for the last $\frac{1}{2}$ mile but there is a wide verge. At the end of the Harlton Road in Haslingfield turn right and continue past the church to Fountain Lane. Turn left and left again at the other end and then right into Cantelupe Road which leads into a footpath to Grantchester. Here the route joins the 10-mile loop back to Cambridge.

The 8½-mile loop from Toft

Whilst not part of the original Oxfam Walk in 1991, we are proposing this circular walk from Toft which uses part of the 20-mile route but does not

involve as much road walking as the original.

Park near to the Post Office in Toft or take the bus to Toft (Stagecoach 18 or 18A).

Walk out of **Toft** in the **Kingston** direction. Just after the road bends right, immediately after a small bridge, turn left and take the footpath to **Kingston** $\frac{3}{4}$ mile. Walk with the stream on your right through a series of x-gates. At a gap in the hedge, to your right, turn right towards a green barn. Beyond the barn the path leads into a lane. At the crossroads in **Kingston** turn left by the Millennium pump. After about 100 yards turn right into Cranes Lane which leads to a wide grassy track. After nearly a mile, don't

Photo by Andy Travers

Millennium Water Pump at Kingston

Photo by Andy Travers

Village Hall at Eversden, used as a checkpoint.

hedge on your right until you reach the concrete water tanks. Carry straight on. Don't turn left or right. Continue for about a mile and turn left, just before a small plantation. Walk downhill to **Little Eversden**.

(At the road, the 20-mile loop turns right to **Harlton** and **Haslingfield**, see above.)

To return to **Toft**, cross the road into the High Street, **Little Eversden**. Opposite Oakwood House turn left through a x-gate. Cross the next lane and go through the x-gate opposite. At the next junction of paths take the right-hand x-gate and do not walk towards the church. The path goes under a beam with the church to your left. After the Village Hall, a former Methodist Chapel, on your right, cross the lane and take the path opposite. After a wooden bridge and another x-gate, the path bears right diagonally across the field. There is a stile just before the road. Turn right and follow the road as it bends left. Go over the stile on the right and follow a wide grassy track between hedges. When you reach a golf course, cross following the blue posts. At the far boundary turn left and continue with the boundary on your right, until you reach a stile. Go over and bear left between trees towards the houses of **Toft**. Go over a small wooden bridge, then a higher bridge. At the road turn left and then right up School Lane back to the Post Office in **Toft**.

go over the bridge ahead and don't turn right, but continue as the path narrows. At the road, turn left past houses. Immediately after the right-bend follow the wooden public bridleway sign into the woods, on the left. Gradually you emerge from the woods onto a grassy track. Keep the

1992

CAMBRIDGE – ADDENBROOKE'S – WANDLEBURY – BABRAHAM – STAPLEFORD – GREAT SHELFORD – CAMBRIDGE

Distance   16 or 8 miles
Map   OS Explorer 209

In 1992 the route directions started at Cambridge University Press sports pavilion but the beginning stages used some paths which were not on public rights of way. The original routes were 12 or 20 miles.

The route featured here has a total distance of approximately 16 miles and starts and finishes at the Trumpington Road end of Brooklands Avenue, Cambridge (see the route in white on the map opposite).

The Roman Road from Wort's Causeway

Photo by David Cutting

The 16-mile route

Follow the signpost 'Public footpath to Long Road' until you reach Long Road. Here turn left and proceed along Long Road for less than ½ mile, then turn right into Robinson Way. Follow the road for ⅔ mile until you meet a sharp bend.

Here, bear right over a verge, through a narrow gate to Red Cross Lane. In about 200 yards you come to the A1307. Cross at the traffic lights, turn right: then second left, marked '**Fulbourn**' and '**Wort's Causeway**'. Continue along Wort's Causeway for about 1½ miles until you reach a footpath junction right onto **Roman Road**. Follow Roman Road footpath about a mile to **Wandlebury**.

(At this point in 1992 the routes diverted to a checkpoint at **Wandlebury** Schoolroom. Those walking the shorter distance returned to Cambridge the way they had come. Those walking the longer distance returned to the Roman Road and continued to Mount Farm.)

Continue for two more miles along the Roman Road to Mount Farm and **Worsted Lodge**.

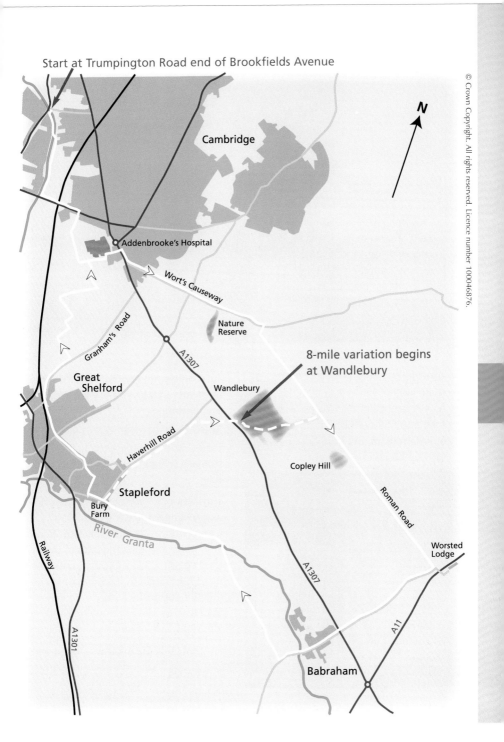

Start at Trumpington Road end of Brookfields Avenue

N

Cambridge

Addenbrooke's Hospital

Wort's Causeway

Nature Reserve

Granham's Road

A1307

Great Shelford

Wandlebury

8-mile variation begins at Wandlebury

Haverhill Road

Copley Hill

Roman Road

Stapleford

Bury Farm

River Granta

Railway

A1301

A1307

A11

Worsted Lodge

Babraham

Rowley Lane between Babraham and Stapleford

Turn right, do not cross A11, but walk south-west for over 1 mile to the A1307. Go straight across the main road and follow right-hand pavement into **Babraham**, over the bridge to Rowley Lane on your right.

Three generations on the 1992 Oxfam Walk

Turn right onto the track and continue for nearly 3 miles to Bury Farm gate, **Stapleford**.

At the road turn left, then, after 200 yards, right into Bar Lane to the primary school (a checkpoint on the day).

Turn left into Vicarage Lane, then right along Mingle Lane to Hinton Way. Cross Hinton Way into Chaston Road and at the end take the path to the level crossing. Go right up Granhams Road for ½ mile to the footpath junction, opposite a mirror. Turn left. Take way-marked path going right, left, right, left, ⅔ mile to Nine Wells.

At Nine Wells turn left through a wide gap in the hedge, then immediately right and continue straight on for 150 yards to a tarmac track. Turn right and

> **An excerpt from the publicity for the 1992 walk:**
>
> Your time and sponsorship money will help Wollayta villagers dig wells and improve existing ones to help remove the risks of disease and water shortage; for example:
>
> £2.60 pays for a bag of cement.
> £5.70 pays for a well-mason's daily wage.
> £50 pays for a mason's tool kit.
> £498 pays for a new handpump.

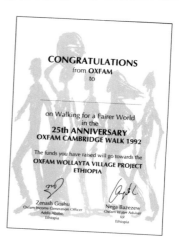

CONGRATULATIONS
from OXFAM
to

on Walking for a Fairer World
in the
25th ANNIVERSARY
OXFAM CAMBRIDGE WALK 1992

The funds you have raised will go towards the
**OXFAM WOLLAYTA VILLAGE PROJECT
ETHIOPIA**

Zenash Goshu
Oxfam Income Generation Officer
Addis Ababa,
Ethiopia

Nega Bazezew
Oxfam Water Adviser
for
Ethiopia

continue for approximately ⅓ mile. Turn left at the bridge. Ahead 250 yards to Robinson Way. Turn left.

Complete the 16-mile route by returning, via Long Road, to Brooklands Avenue.

An 8-mile variation on the original

This variation is shown by the dashed white line on the map on page 47, starting at Wandlebury car park, joining the original route to the east on the Roman Road, following the southern loop of the original route and then splitting from it at Stapleford to return to Wandlebury. This is approximately 8 miles.

From the Wandlebury Car Park Follow the footpaths to the Roman Road and turn right onto the Roman Road.

Continue for two more miles along the Roman Road to Mount Farm and **Worsted Lodge**.

Turn right, do not cross A11, but walk south-west for over 1 mile to the A1307. Go straight across the main road and follow right-hand pavement into **Babraham**, over the bridge to Rowley Lane on your right.

Turn right onto the track and continue for nearly 3 miles to Bury Farm gate, **Stapleford**.

Turn right along the pavement for nearly 1½ miles. Turn onto the footpath across the Magog Trust land, signposted **Wandlebury** ½ mile.

Walk over the rise and when you reach the dual carriageway cross to the **Wandlebury** car park.

Photo by David Cutting

Rowley Lane from Babraham as it reaches Bury Farm

1996

LINTON – HILDERSHAM – ABINGTON – BABRAHAM – STAPLEFORD – WANDLEBURY

Distance   9 miles
Map   OS Explorer 209

The 1996 route

In 1996 the route started at Stapleford Primary School and consisted of 14- and 7-mile sections to Linton or a complete 21 mile loop, via Wandlebury. The route from Wandlebury to Linton, via Fulbourn and Balsham, is the same as that described in the 1974 route (see pages 25–27). The full 21 miles can be achieved by continuing with the 9-mile route described below.

Photo by Andy Travers

En route from Hildersham to Abington

9-mile route from Linton to Wandlebury via Stapleford

If you are continuing from the 12-mile route, cross the High Street bridge in Linton. If you are starting from Linton there is usually parking in the High Street. If you are arriving by bus, get off at 'the Swan', Linton, and cross the High Street bridge. Bus No.13, Cambridge – Haverhill via Linton, stops at Wandlebury.

Walk down Meadow Lane, by the 'Dog and Duck', and along the left side of the recreation ground, leaving by the 'clapper stile'. Walk between railed paddocks to the barns at **Little Linton**. Cross the small access road and walk

at first between hedges. The path skirts Cow Gallery Wood and the sewage works on your left and then takes the right-hand edge of two successive fields. After a paddock on the left, cross over the concrete track and 100 yards later, go through a gate on the right. Cross a narrow bridge and bear to the left to reach **Hildersham's** low wooden village hall. At the road, cross, turn right and immediately after the bridge turn left through a gate. Walk with the river on your left, cross the white bridge and continue over the fields towards the A1307, passing through a narrow belt of trees. Cross the main road at West Lodge Kennels. Go though the gate opposite and turn right towards **Abington**. Turn left at the thatched 1908 house and walk down the right-hand pavement. Turn towards St. Mary's Church. Pass the church on your left and continue to a green bridge. Cross and follow a narrow footpath to reach the road. Cross and turn left. Follow this road as it bends right and left, leaving the village along a straight section. Turn right at the road junction and then turn left to cross the A11 by footbridge. Continue with the hedge on your right to **Babraham**. Cross the High Street. Turn left and then right, at a gap in the flint wall (Stapleford $2\frac{1}{2}$ m). Go over a bridge and along the tarmac track with the river on your right. Go through two metal X-gates and then along a cross-field path. (You continue in this direction to **Stapleford**). After a mixed planting of young trees, turn right and left, with field on the left and woods to your right. At the end of the fence, turn right and then left, to walk along a grassy track, through a small plantation. After a X-gate turn right onto a bridle-path. Cross the bridge and turn left between two concrete posts, to walk along the left-hand edge of the field. Continue until you reach the Haverhill Road, **Stapleford**. Turn right along the pavement which gives way to a footpath in the verge, signposted to Linton and Haverhill. After a concrete drive, before the brow of the hill, turn onto the footpath across the Magog Trust land, Wandlebury $\frac{1}{2}$ m. Carry straight on over the hill and when you reach the dual carriageway cross over to **Wandlebury** car park.

Start at Linton High Street

1997

WHITTLESFORD – THRIPLOW – FOWLMERE – FOXTON – NEWTON – WHITTLESFORD

Distance   7, 14 or 21 miles (originally) 11½ -mile alternative proposal
Map   OS Explorer 209

West Hill, on the path from Fowlmere to Foxton

The 1997 original route

The original routes were from Whittlesford via Foxton to Melbourn (14 miles), Whittlesford via Thriplow to Melbourn (7 miles) or the two combined (21 miles). Three quite long sections were on private paths and the only alternative routes involve long stretches of roads. The western end included a very pleasant path from the A10 to Barrington and a stroll along the river Mel from Meldreth church to Melbourn.

On the map opposite, the original route is shown by the dotted white

line but parts of this are no longer available. The variation we offer is the route described below shown by the solid white line. This is a circular walk from Whittlesford to Thriplow and Fowlmere, returning via Foxton and Newton and gives a section of the eastern end of the original route.

Whittlesford to Fowlmere and back via Newton (11½ miles)

From **Whittlesford** school go across the recreation ground to the opposite corner. Cross the road and at the Guildhall turn left into the High Street, walking past the post office. Continue along West End to Hill Farm Road. At the junction turn left and after the last house on the left, before the brow of the hill, turn right to **Thriplow** 1½. Cross the M11 bridge and continue along the track, the Drift, to Thriplow, bearing right at the fork just before you reach the village. When you reach the road turn right and take the footpath on the left, into a field, leaving by a gate to the far right. Walk along a narrow path between chain link fences to the road. Go right along Middle Street and turn left at School Lane to follow the pavement to

Photo by David Cutting

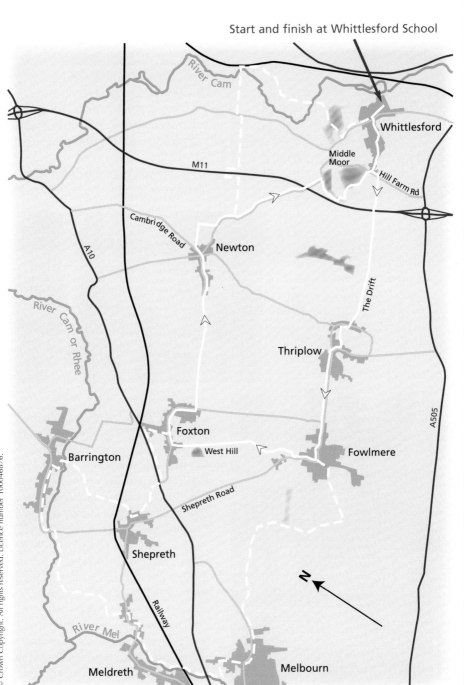

Start and finish at Whittlesford School

Whittlesford

Middle Moor

M11

Hill Farm Rd

Cambridge Road

Newton

The Drift

Thriplow

Foxton

West Hill

Fowlmere

Barrington

Shepreth Road

Shepreth

Railway

River Mel

Meldreth

Melbourn

A10

A505

River Cam

River Cam or Rhee

The village of Foxton

the right, continue along cross-field paths and then between plantations of young trees before you reach Caxton Lane, **Foxton**. Turn right and follow the High Street round for nearly ½ mile. Turn left onto a footpath, just before a phone box. Walk with a hedge to your left, cross a concrete bridge and continue with a brook to your right until you reach Town Street, **Newton**. At the Queen's Head turn left

Fowlmere, where you turn right at the War Memorial. Walk along the road to **Shepreth** out of **Fowlmere**. Take the footpath to the right signed '**Foxton 1½**, after 'Seven Elms'. Walk for a short distance on a narrow path between houses. Turn left onto a cross-field path. Go over a bridge to

Middle Moor on the approach to Whittlesford.

onto the Cambridge Road and just before the end of the village look for a signed footpath on the right. Follow this track which bends right half way along and comes out on the Whittlesford Road out of Newton. Turn left and walk along the road or the verge for just over a mile. The road crosses the M11 and shortly after you will see a track signed through woods on the right. Take this path as it curves through the woods going over a bridge, to emerge along the left-hand side of a field. Go over the stile and turn right at Whippletree Road and then left into West End. Retrace the beginning part of the walk to Whittlesford School.

1998

WIMPOLE HALL – THE EVERSDENS – KINGSTON WOOD –
HAYLEY WOOD – HATLEY ST GEORGE – CROYDON –
ARRINGTON – WIMPOLE HALL

Distance   7, 14 or 21 miles
Maps   OS Explorer 208 and 209

The lake at Wimpole Hall

Wimpole to the Eversdens and back (7 miles)

The route is shown on our map by the dashed white line and is on OS Explorer 209.

From the Stable Block, Wimpole, walk down the drive until you reach the first field on the left. Go through the gate and walk diagonally across two fields to reach the road. Cross and follow the track opposite, to a small bridge and through the farm yard of Cobb's Wood Farm. Continue up the incline, passing woods and then a hedge on your left. At the fork of two paths go left and past a small group of trees. At the junction of four paths, just before the concrete water towers, go right, signposted to **Little Eversden**. Follow the Mare Way, along the chalk ridge, for just under a mile and take the first track on the left down to the Eversdens. When you meet the fork of three paths, take the middle one bearing left between trees and at the field go right, down to the road. Cross and go left and then right down Bucks Lane. Just before Five Gables Farm turn left through a swing gate, turning right towards the **Village Hall**, *not* the church. At the road beyond the Village Hall turn left, then right at the Hoops, continuing down the High Street. As the road bends to the right, just before Manor Farm on the left, cross and pass to the left-hand side of the gate and go over the stile, over a little bridge and follow the way-marked path uphill, with the barbed wire fence to your right. Pass an isolated tree and go over the stile, at the end of the field, then straight on until the path meets the ditch at right angles. Turn left and continue, with the ditch on your left, until you reach **Eversden Wood**. Take the right-hand track following the edge of the Wood, until you reach the way-marked entrance to the Wood straight ahead. Go through the Wood to the T-junction of paths. Turn left and after a little way, turn right to the edge of the Wood and then right again along a path between the Wood and a hedge to your left. After about 250 yards, at a wide gap in the hedge, turn left diagonally across the field and at the other side turn right towards the road. Turn left for approx. 200 yards and then left into the woods, the Gloucesters, and follow the path through the woods. At the end of the woods turn right down the hill and retrace your steps to Wimpole Hall.

Photo by David Cutting

Hayley Wood

Wimpole to Hayley Wood and back through Hatley St George and Croydon (14 miles)

The route is shown on our map by the solid white line and begins on OS Explorer map 209. From the Stable Block, Wimpole, walk north through the park, over the Chinese Bridge and past the Folly to your right. Continue and turn right at the woods, the Belts. Where the path emerges at the road, turn left and follow the road round to New Farm. After the second house turn right along the signed footpath. After $\frac{1}{2}$ mile turn left onto a bridleway. At the junction of paths turn right and after another $\frac{1}{3}$ mile turn left towards **Kingston Wood**. Change maps to OS Explorer 208. When you reach Kingston Wood

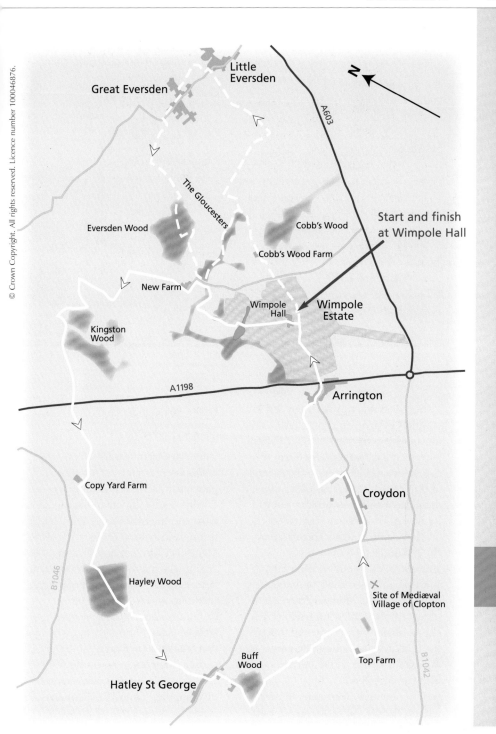

Great Eversden

Little Eversden

A603

The Gloucesters

Eversden Wood

Cobb's Wood

Start and finish at Wimpole Hall

Cobb's Wood Farm

New Farm

Wimpole Hall

Wimpole Estate

Kingston Wood

A1198

Arrington

Copy Yard Farm

Croydon

B1046

Hayley Wood

Site of Mediæval Village of Clopton

Buff Wood

Top Farm

B1042

Hatley St George

Photo by David Cutting

The site of Clopton Mediæval village. This was a flourishing village until the fifteenth century. The Romans were here nearly 2,000 years ago. The Anglo-Saxons built a village here which was well-established by Domesday, with two manors and at least 19 households. Two centuries later, between 5 – 600 people lived here.

follow the footpath with the wood to your left. When you reach the T-junction with a wide track, the Porters' Way, turn left and walk for about a mile to the A1198. Cross and continue to Copy Yard Farm. The track turns left at the farm and you continue along a bridleway which turns right, after under ½ mile towards **Hayley Wood**. Go into and across the wood to emerge on the south-western side. Turn left and then almost immediately right and after a little way turn left at some farm buildings. After 200 yards, approximately, turn right and follow the bridleway to **Hatley St George**. At the road turn left and then right into Buff Lane for about ½ mile. (You may be lucky enough to see deer in the wood). Turn left at the corner of **Buff Wood**, with the wood to your left. Continue straight on at the top of the wood. After about a mile from the wood turn right towards Top Farm, where you turn left. At X-roads of paths turn left onto the Clopton Way. Continue past the site of the Mediæval village to the road. Cross and walk through Croydon Village to the War Memorial. Turn left, uphill, and continue along the Clopton Way. Do not turn into Manor farm but follow the footpath as it bears right. Continue, *dogs on leads past the modern house to the left*, and when you reach **Arrington**, turn right to the church, then left to reach the A1198. Cross, and go through the back gates of **Wimpole** – almost 1 mile to the stable block.

2004

CHILFORD HALL – HILDERSHAM – LINTON – HADSTOCK

Distance   7, 14 or 21 miles (originally) here, two $6\frac{1}{2}$-mile variations
              are proposed

Maps   OS Explorer 209

The routes devised in 2004 of 7, 14 and 21 miles, included some stretches of private land for which special permission was obtained to use them on the day. As these parts are no longer accessible to the public, we are proposing two $6\frac{1}{2}$-mile walks that are mostly part of the original routes, with variations where necessary.

Bruce Kent setting off in 2004.

Roman Road via Hildersham ($6\frac{1}{2}$-mile circular walk)

This route is very similar to the 8-mile route used in 2006 (see page 63) but does not include Chilford drive or the back drive to the barns. To be close to the original route it is described from a start at the bend of the B1052 just before Chilford Drive (and shown on the map on page 61 by the dashed white line). It could be started from Hildersham or Linton if coming by bus.

Walk along the verge of the B1052 to just beyond the Chilford Drive and take a signed cross-field path, through the hedge, on the right-hand side of the road. Cross two fields to reach the Harcamlow Way (Roman Road) and turn left. The track crosses the B1052 and after nearly a mile crosses the

Hildersham to Balsham Road. Continue for just under a mile to where the hedge on the left stops and there is a fine view across the Granta valley. Turn left down a grassy track and turn right when you meet the road. Continue, with care, to cross the cross-roads to **Hildersham**. Walk through the village and over the bridge until you reach the low, wooden village hall on your left. Go through a small gate just before the village hall and follow the path with the river on your left, past a bridge and across a second field to a X-gate just before **Hildersham Mill**. Turn right and walk along the drive until

Photo by Mike Crofts

On the way to Hadstock checkpoint

you reach a left turn onto a track, before a railed paddock. Follow this path, past the barns of **Little Linton** on your left, then between railed paddocks to the Clapper Stile at **Linton** recreation ground. Follow the path to the left to the white bridge. Cross and take the path to the road, Symonds Lane. Cross and go straight on between metal posts to the path opposite. Keep to the right. At the T-junction turn right, then left to cross the road and take the Icknield Way path uphill, just beyond the telephone exchange. Follow this path past the water tower, after which turn left to return to where the track meets the B1052.

Chilford to Linton and Hadstock (6$\frac{1}{2}$-mile circular walk)

The 14-mile circular route crossed the Essex border to Little Walden and back via Hadstock. Special permission was given for two sections over private land. Therefore the complete route is not described here but a shortened circular walk is proposed (shown by the solid white line).

Start at the bend of the B1052 just before Chilford drive. There is room for one or two cars to park off the road. Walk up the bridleway signposted Icknield Way and follow the track round to the right past the water tower, then left down hill

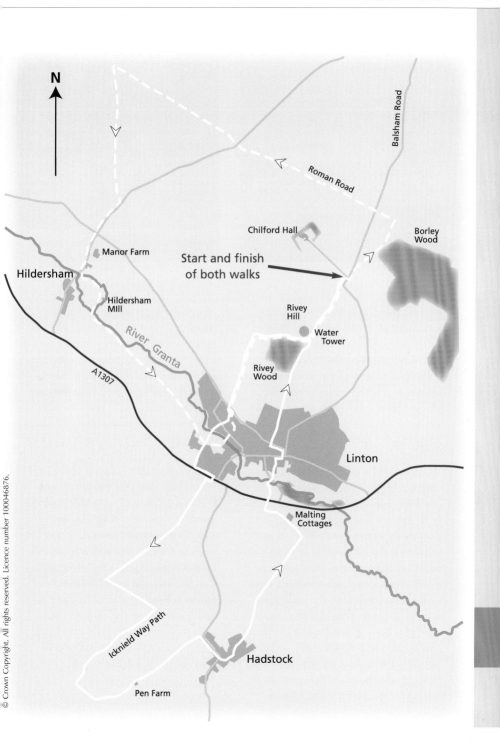

The village of Hadstock and walkers passing through in 2004.

beyond the woods. At the road, cross, turn right and then left into Crabtree Croft. Keep on the pavement to the left. Cross the next road, Symonds Lane, and walk on a path between houses to a white bridge. Continue straight ahead to a path, past **Linton** village college, to the A1307. Turn left and cross the main road at the pedestrian crossing, then walk back to the bus shelter. Take the footpath just beyond as it goes over two stiles and continue with the hedge on your left to a slightly raised path bearing diagonally right across a field. When you reach the hedge turn left and very soon left again with a ditch to your right. When you reach another hedge turn right onto a path through trees. Continue on the Icknield Way and just after you have walked under overhead cables, turn left. Walk for nearly a mile past Pen Farm. Turn right at the road through **Hadstock**. At the green, turn left up the hill. Turn left at Moules Lane to the recreation ground. Cross

diagonally to the far left corner and take the path slightly uphill towards **Linton**. At the top carry straight on but with the hedge on your right, bearing right at the bottom, then left over a disused railway bridge. Bear left past Maltings cottages. Do not turn right when you come to the road but continue beyond the turning and look for a gap in the hedge and a cross-field path to the A1307. Cross and continue on the path towards the white mill buildings. Go over the bridge, bear left under the mill and then diagonally right to a footpath between walls. This leads to Green Lane which leads to **Linton** High Street. Turn right at the Co-op, cross and turn left into Balsham Road, and then left into Back Road. Just before the cemetery turn right to the footpath on the opposite side of the road and walk along the Icknield Way back to the start.

2006

BALSHAM – WEST WICKHAM – HORSEHEATH – BALSHAM

Distance   4, 8, 15, 21 or 26 miles (originally) here, an 11-mile variation is proposed

Maps   OS Explorer 209 and 210

The original walks in 2006

The **8-mile** loop was similar to the 7-mile loop for 2004 (see page 59).

The **4-mile** loop is not described here because it went through private woods.

The **15-mile** route started at Chilford Hall and followed the same route to the Roman Road as the 8-mile route or the 7-mile route of 2004. But at the Roman Road the 15-milers turned right for nearly ½ mile, turning left onto the Icknield Way for nearly 1½ miles before reaching the thatched butcher's shop at the end of Woodhall Lane in Balsham. The route then turned left down the High Street, right along Nine Chimneys Lane, left and then right along the Icknield Way and returned to **Balsham** recreation ground and the church along the Harcamlow Way. (There is parking at the post office end of Woodhall Lane.)

The Roman Road

Photo by Carrie travers

Mark's Grave – Harcamlow Way

Photo by Carrie travers

Our proposal of an 11-mile variation

Part of the 15-mile route can be walked as an 11-mile circular walk from Balsham, via West Wickham and Horseheath.

From the post office in **Balsham** cross the High Street and walk along the lane opposite as it turns right towards the church joining the 15-mile route. Walk through the churchyard, taking the right fork to School Lane. At the end, cross and turn left and then right at the gate sign-posted **West Wratting**

1¼. Follow the path over two foot bridges and round the right-hand edge of the next field to the far corner, leaving the field at some wooden steps. Turn right along the edge of the field to overhead cables where you turn left across the fields to woodland. Go through the wood and continue across the field, turning left at the far hedge to reach Padlock Road. Turn right and right again at the T-junction. Take the footpath on the left, beyond a large barn and follow the left-hand edge of the field, heading towards **West Wickham**. Midway down the

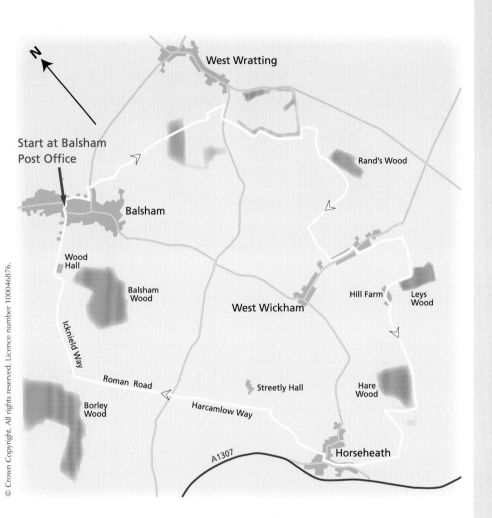

field turn left and then right onto a concrete path which you follow through a belt of trees. The path turns into a wide grassy track, between fields. Turn left beyond another belt of trees and after about 100 yards, turn right and follow the edge of the field with the hedge on your left. Exit the field at a narrow way-marked gap in the hedge and bear right over a footbridge. Follow the left-hand edges of

two fields, past Rands Wood, until you come to a meeting of several paths. Cross the footbridge straight ahead and turn sharp right. Walk along the right-hand edge of two fields and then turn left uphill. At an intersection take the path to the right and after 50 yards turn left through a gap in the hedge to walk past **West Wickham** village hall. Turn left at the road for about 200 yards, cross and at the public footpath

Photo by Carrie Travers

West Wickham

sign, turn right to go through a small wooden gate. When the path forks, bear left and follow the path through a gap in the trees. To your left there are trees and later a ditch. Do not cross the footbridge but take the cross-field path to your right. Cross a very narrow footbridge and turn immediately right to walk between trees. Continue, eventually bearing right to emerge from the trees. Further on, the path turns into a concrete track. After a 100 yards turn sharp left, when the hedge ends, and walk between barns. Take a right fork and follow a broad cross-field path towards a hedge. Carry straight on uphill, towards a line of trees. At the top turn right through a gap in the hedge, then left to a cross-field path to Hare Wood. (*Here there were extensions for the marathon route which are not described.*) Continue along the path with the wood to your right and at the end of the wood turn right onto a gravel track. After about 400

yards turn left across the field towards woodland and then down a wide grassy track. At overhead cables turn right across two fields towards the houses of **Horseheath**. At the road, turn right and go past the village hall, to turn right by a garage. At the next road cross to Audley Way. Follow the right-hand pavement and bear right after No.18. Go through a wooden X-gate and follow the right-hand edge of the field. Go through another X-gate, over a bridge and turn left to continue along a bank with a ditch on your right. The path bends right. At an iron-barred gate turn left onto the Roman Road. Continue for about 1½ miles to the right turn along the Icknield Way to Balsham. Follow this byway for about 1½ miles back to **Balsham**.

(The 15-mile route continued back to Chilford along the Roman Road and through private woods.)

Eager walkers registering in 2002

Behind the scenes

You may imagine, and with very good reason, that organising the Oxfam Walk involves a great deal of work. We thought readers might be interested in just how much work is required and what takes place behind the scenes to bring about this event each year.

The organising committee, comprising some 20 people, begin regular monthly meetings in September which increase to fortnightly meetings after New Year. The committee are all volunteers who give their time freely to co-ordinate the tasks that need to be done. There are approximately another 200 volunteers who help in many varied ways with whatever time they can spare in the preparation of the event and on the day of the walk.

As early as August, Oxfam send out a recruitment letter inviting previous walkers to volunteer to help with the event next year. By September

the venue for the start of the walk has been booked and the routes have been devised. A budget is set and agreed with Oxfam.

It is the job of the Walk Co-ordinator to ensure that all the marketing and logistical functions of the walk are managed and are done on schedule and the treasurer co-ordinates the budget and produces monthly accounts to be approved by the team and then sent to Oxfam House.

At the first committee meeting the members are asked to agree who will fill the various co-ordinating roles. A diverse range of skills are required! The many jobs that need to be done fall into three main categories: logistics, marketing and sponsors. The following list of roles gives an indication of the extent of the work that is necessary.

Banner in Sydney Street, Cambridge

Logistics

Routes co-ordinator: Responsible for designing the route and identifying checkpoints on the routes and, with the AA, organising the Traffic Management Plan.

Health and safety: A risk assessment has to be written and this co-ordinator liaises with Oxfam House over all other Health & Safety documents.

Safety team co-ordinator: Liaises with the safety team (Red Cross, Special Police and Raynet communications network). Sends a courtesy letter to landowners and a letter to the Streetworks team. The routes are checked with the County Council Countryside Services Team.

Route directions: It is most important that unambiguous route directions are written for all the walk options and these are tested by people not involved in the design of the routes or the writing of the directions to ensure they are understandable to a walker following the route for the first time.

Route signage and banner: Two banners are put up, one for Sidney Street and the other in a major satellite town. Several teams are allocated different sections of the route and each team must walk their section and decide what signs will be needed. The co-ordinator then organises the production of the signs so that there are enough arrows, marshal numbers, route signs and checkpoint signs.

Signing teams co-ordinator: Co-ordinates the teams erecting the direction signs on the day before the walk and removing them afterwards.

Equipment and landowner co-ordinators (two people): Organise equipment for the checkpoints, signing equipment and signing teams. Most of the equipment is in storage.

Checkpoints and catering: Organises the checkpoints and catering groups at each checkpoint.

Marshals co-ordinator (logistics): Confirms marshal points and draws the marshal point map. This co-ordinator also writes and draws the individual hand-drawn marshal maps and road access map. They are also responsible for calculating the distances and safety timings around the route.

Marshals co-ordinator (recruitment): Over 100 marshals and stewards need to be recuited and their timetables written. This Co-ordinator organises the marshal and steward packs and liaises with the cadets who steward the car park.

Marketing

Evaluation co-ordinator: Each year we prepare an evaluation form and analyse the data after the walk.

Oxfam shops and schools: Liaising with the Oxfam shops and sending them posters and registration forms to display. A promotional mailing is also sent to all the local schools.

Photo opportunities: This picture of Tanya Simpson, Basic Rights Campaign Co-ordinator for Oxfam, and George Kent, appeared in The Cambridge Evening News on 25 April 1997, heading an article about "a mystery cake cutting ceremony". Readers were invited to identify where the picture was taken and Oxfam Walk t-shirts were offered as prizes.

Media (articles and press releases): The media co-ordinator (articles) helps devise a media plan and writes articles for newspapers and radio from early March until the day of the Walk.

Media co-ordinator (media liaison): Helps devise the media plan, liaises with the media and arranges for photo opportunities to accompany articles (photo call). It is also the job of this co-

ordinator to find a celebrity to launch the walk in March and arrange radio interviews.

Webpage, Oxfam team trophy/ marathon walk: This job requires co-ordinating the Oxfam Walk webpage, part of Oxfam's website, and also promoting the Oxfam Team Trophy and the marathon walk to businesses.

Exhibitions co-ordinator: Organises materials from Oxfam to be used in exhibitions at each checkpoint depicting Oxfam's work and the project the Oxfam Walk is supporting.

Pre-walk party: Each year there is a pre-walk party held for all walkers, sponsors and marshals & stewards. This gives everyone involved the opportunity to meet each other and to learn more about how the walk helps the work of Oxfam.

Publications: The publications co-ordinator writes and sends articles to parish newsletters and other publications and organises an exhibition of walk materials in the Central Library. S/he writes a courtesy letter to parish councils.

A promotional display mounted by volunteers in 1998

Photo courtesy of Cambridge Evening News

Statistics co-ordinator: Statistics from registration forms and entry cards are collated after the walk and this information can be used for marketing purposes for the following year.

Sponsors

Donations in kind: There are approximately 12 sponsors who give or lend us donations in kind and it is very important to have someone responsible for liaising with them.

Entertainers: Liaises with about six entertainers who give their time for free on the day of the walk.

Countdown to the big day

By the end of November the route map is confirmed and permission from private landowners has been sought with a courtesy letter sent to all other landowners. Permission is also obtained from Ordnance Survey for paper and internet maps. Catering teams are found and the Council distribution Service and the exhibition

area at the Central Library is booked.

By Christmas, all our sponsors are confirmed and materials such as the letter for the past walker mailing, poster, registration form and entrants' pack have been written. The website is agreed and a t-shirt designed. The route map is sent to both the Streetworks Department and the Countryside Services Team at the County Council who ensure that any streetworks en route are properly signed and check that we are aware of all private paths.

In January around 30 marshal points along all the routes are confirmed and a publicity article is sent to Parish newsletters. All the checkpoint sites are visited and by February the risk assessment, safety plan, emergencies procedures and safety timings are written. A meeting with the Red Cross and Raynet (communications network) confirms further safety measures around the route. The walk webpage on the Oxfam website goes live.

By March things are really hotting up as the Oxfam Walk is officially launched by a celebrity with a press release in the local media. A huge team of marshals and stewards begins to be assembled and duty timetables are prepared. A map for each marshal detailing their position is drawn and the timings from each start point to each marshal point are established. Also the signing teams are confirmed and a traffic management plan is drawn up. 11,000 registration forms and 1,000 posters are distributed by the walk team and the banner goes up

The t-shirt design to celebrate the walk's 40th anniversary in 2007

in central Cambridge and a major satellite town. An article is emailed to free listings and magazines, a letter is sent to Parish councils notifying them of the walk, 25 Oxfam shops display walk materials and a mailing is sent to schools.

In April marketing continues with a mailing to Parish councils and press releases and radio interviews are organised. The cadets who are helping with the parking are sent a reminder and a final parking plan and sponsors are reminded of what they have offered to do.

A signing team preparing the route in 1999

The signing teams complete their reconnoitre of the route and submit their reports about the signs required. The final route directions are sent to Oxfam for printing. All health and safety documents are distributed and checkpoint leaders and deputies are briefed. The central co-ordination plan and registration procedures are finalised. Checkpoint and signing equipment is checked and sorted.

The Walk

Two days before the walk, items are collected from all over Cambridge and there is a briefing for signing teams, checkpoint leaders and deputies. The day before the walk five signing teams gather at 9.30am to collect their equipment and go out to put up the direction signs along the routes.

The day of the walk begins at 5.00am when a walk team member with the AA, puts up road signs around the routes. At 6.00am, a team of volunteers arrives at the start/finish

point. This is a very busy time as tables for registration, facepainters, foot masseurs, t-shirts, books, Children's Corner, Oxfam Local Campaigns Group and the Oxfam Shop are arranged.

The caterers set up and a thousand bottles of water are brought in. Exhibition boards, covered with Oxfam materials, are put up and more signs and banners are erected outside. Space is made available for the band. Tents are put up for the Red Cross and the sports masseur. The cadets arrive to steward the car park. Everything has to be ready by 8.00am for registration.

Meanwhile, marshals in distinctive fluorescent vests are getting into position along the route, a team of cyclists are biking round the routes checking that direction signs are still in place and checkpoint leaders with their deputies, Red Cross personnel and refreshments teams are setting up their checkpoints ready for the first walkers.

Throughout the day, the trouble-shooting vehicle patrols the routes responding to requests from the event co-ordinator and checkpoint leaders. The photographer takes photos to be used in future Oxfam Walk publicity, the Woodcraft Folk play parachute games with the children outside the start/finish point and the press arrive to take photos for the local media.

At the checkpoints blisters are tended and encouragement is imbibed with tea and cake. Aching limbs are rested and thirsty dogs are refreshed.

As registration desks close, backmarkers follow walkers round the routes dismissing marshals and collecting direction signs.

At the end of the day, 4 x 4 vehicles drive round the routes collecting the stakes which the backmarkers left at the stake dumps and all the equipment from the checkpoints is returned to storage. The start/finish point is cleared up and everyone heaves a huge sigh of relief. Another walk well done!

The Oxfam Walk runs smoothly because all 200 volunteers are well briefed and do their job thoroughly. Foreseeable problems are anticipated so that if, for example, a marshal drops out on the day, a 'floating' marshal is

A checkpoint on the 1997 walk

sent out from the start/finish point. The troubleshooting vehicle is available throughout the day to deal with challenges along the route. Walkers are given a telephone number to ring in case of emergency and all volunteers are briefed as to what to do in an emergency.

Clean water, sanitation, food, shelter, medical care and protection have been available to all the walkers. Their many thousands of steps taken will be converted into clean water, sanitation, medical care and hope for people affected by global disasters.

It's a big day. But for everyone involved – almost 2,000 volunteers and walkers working towards a common aim – it's been worth it!

The Oxfam Walk has become a part of the Cambridge landscape. When you take part in the Walk you feel that you are part of a community, and it's a powerful experience. You are having a fun day out, of course. But you also feel that you are joining hundreds of like-minded people who also want to express their shared commitment to a cause. Coming together in this way, we are, in the words of the old development slogan, 'thinking globally, acting locally.'

Julian Jacobs, Oxfam's Regional Campaigns Manager in the 1990s